Journey Unexpected

Navigating Life After College

Andrea D. Boyd

Paperback: 978-0-9600273-1-6

eBook: 978-0-9600273-2-3

www.Simplydrea.com

This book is dedicated to:

My Mommy:
You are one of the strongest women I know and I thank you for your endless love, support and for showing me what a strong woman of God truly looks like! Your strength, courage and selflessness are traits that I admire about you. I love you more than I can even begin to describe. Thank you for all of the sacrifices you made for me.

My Grandma:
Also known as my #1 hero! You were the definition of strength and kindness. When I saw you I saw God shining His light through one of His greatest creations. With all you went through, I never once saw you sweat. I thank you for the God-fearing mentality you instilled in me. You had the most genuine and loving spirit and I truly wish to be like you when I get older.

My Family:
Who would I be without my family?! Thank you all for surrounding me with your love and molding me into the person I am today.
Knowing I have such a strong and powerful support system is truly amazing.

Recent College Grads:
This book is for you! I believe that my stories and pain are not just for me but for people needing to hear that I made it through. Whatever storm you are facing know that, with God by your side, you can get through it all! I love you all, keep pushing because it gets better!

More from

Andrea Deniise

Check out and subscribe to her
Youtube Channel!

Youtube.com/SimplyDrea

@DreaDeniise

www.SimplyDrea.com/AList
Join her email list also known as the
A List for weekly tips, motivation, and
encouragement

More from

Andrea Denise

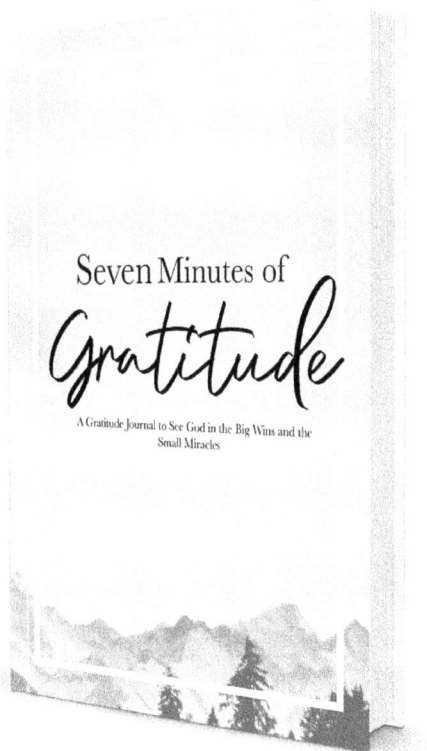

Seven Minutes of Gratitude is a journal
to help us focus on all God is doing in and
through our daily lives. I truly believe that a
grateful heart leads to endless opportunities
and opens doors no man can shut!
www.SimplyDrea.com

Contents

Chapter 1:
The Journey Begins

Chapter 2:
Holding on to My College Days

Chapter 3:
Is There a Class on Adulting?

Chapter 4:
The Waiting Season

Chapter 5:
My Blessing in Disguise

Chapter 6:
Here God, Take Back This Wheel

Chapter 7:
Teach Me to Trust You

Chapter 1:

The Journey Begins

*"You have searched me, Lord, and you know me.
You know when I sit and when I rise; you perceive
my thoughts from afar. You discern my going out and
my lying down; you are familiar with all my ways."*
– Psalm 139: 1-3

Let's be honest, as much as we like to think
we have life all figured out, deep down we know
that couldn't be further from the truth. During a
life transition, the thought of what's next can be
terrifying due to the unknown! If we compare
ourselves with our environment, it may look like
EVERYONE around us has their life map and plan

ready for action, but I'm here to tell you this is not the case! It's not even close.

Hi, I'm Andrea or as my friends and subscribers call me, Drea (Dray-UH). I'm a recent college graduate of the amazing University of Missouri, and I'm here to tell you that it is okay not to have it all together after college. In fact, many graduates do not have a clue of what lies ahead right after they grab their well earned diploma either. Now, this is not me giving you permission to slack off and be lazy about your future. However it is me telling you to relax and take a deep breath if you feel like a blind fish out of water with no since of direction.

I assure you that you are not alone, my friend - you will make it through this wilderness just as many of us have.

If you are currently stuck in this weird lull of time between college and the working world, know that no matter if you have secured a job after graduation, still praying for one, moving far away, heading back home, or anything in between – it will all work out! Doesn't it always?

When I graduated I needed so badly for

someone who had been where I was going to look me in the eyes and tell me that it is okay not to have my entire life planned to perfection, my first job probably wouldn't be my dream job, and not to freak out and doubt that I'll ever have a job that I love (if you're as dramatic as me, you understand). I needed to know that planning my life out, down to specific ages, dates, and detail was a waste of time considering only God knows the plan for our lives and laughs when we make our own. I needed a good shaking to let me know that though it may not be lillies and roses right now, not to worry, I'll eventually get there!

So my friend, that is what I am here to do for YOU. I am here to be the person that shakes you and lets you know, "…in all things God works for the good of those who love Him, who have been called according to his purpose" Romans 8:28 NIV. Just be patient, diligent and trust in God's timing. After all, He is the one that has been in your tomorrow and knows what is ahead!

Life is going to be very different now that the security blanket of college is gone. Don't worry if you aren't where you thought you would be in life at this time. Use that as motivation to get to where you plan to go! Know that you still have time to get there and that as long as your keep your goals right in front of you and have God right alongside you, you will end up exactly where you need to be!

During my stressful transition out of college, trusting God with my future was honestly not even a thought I had at the time. I was too focused on figuring it all out myself because, quite frankly, I forgot I could ask for His help. I lost hope and was worried that I didn't know which way to go. Looking back and seeing where God has brought me from, I can now tell you in confidence to let God completely take the wheel without you trying to reach over and help Him steer. Take it from me, a girl who started out in a pesky sales marketing position that was sold to her as a awesome marketing opportunity to now working for the most amazing nonprofit organization that serves thousands of children in Africa. If you would have asked me May 14th 2016, where I would be in a years time, never in a million years could I have guessed the blessing God had waiting for me, especially since I came out of college with diploma in hand yet no job in site.

Through my journey, from graduation to today, God has shown me that He is in COMPLETE CONTROL and I am perfectly okay with that…. Now! I've realized that if I let go and trust Him, He'll guide me and who better to guide me than my creator.

Now, in no way am I saying I have it all together and I will never pretend to but what I am saying is, once I stopped stressing about the future and started praying about it, God opened my mind and eyes to what I needed to do next. Once I truly passed it all over to Him, I was able to stop stressing about what was to come and focus on what I could control and work on in the moment. Now that I see what it is like when I actually let God lead, I'll never go back to how I was doing it before!

Krista- 24 years old, 20Something & Living podcast (@20somethingandliving)

Five months after graduation, I was on a high – I was offered a good job with AT&T, about to move to Atlanta (somewhere I always wanted to live), finally losing weight, had a boyfriend and amazing family/friends. At first, Atlanta felt like paradise but I quickly saw things turning.

The guy I was dating really hurt me. I thought I could afford my bills, but couldn't. My superficial coworkers were the main people I knew in the city. And with them, I drank too much and was developing alcoholic tendencies. With the alcohol, came weight gain. Being 8 hours away, showed me I am a huge family person and being away takes a large toll on me.

Atlanta was a temporary move. My job

consisted of a 6 month training where after they'd assign you to another city for 18 months. During the hiring the process, my interviewer didn't make that clear as I told her I would like to stay in Atlanta. And she said that would likely happen. Wrong. My choices were between Minneapolis and Cleveland. They were the same distance from home, so I chose Cleveland. I cried for a week. I considered quitting but I knew I should go. But it still wasn't easy. I was moving to a city I never in my LIFE even wanted to visit, let a lone live. I had no family, friends, acquaintances…literally, no one.

By the time I was settled in Ohio, my depression had gotten much worse – it was everything I felt in Atlanta, plus more with living somewhere I hated with no one to help with me through it. And back then, I would hide my depression from myself and act like it didn't exist. But in July 2015 on a Saturday, a light bulb went off in my head and I told myself I was going to church the next day. That was nothing but God. My dad had told me about a church his friend's mentor preached at, The Word Church, so I looked up times and went. When I walked in, I didn't know I was changing my life.

Since that July, I think I've missed one Sunday at that church. At first, I caught myself religiously going to service. Then I thought, "I should try Bible Study". Soon after, I became a regular at that.

Though I had always been a Christian, church was teaching me to do the Christian thing and let God lead my life. I obviously couldn't do it myself. The first thing, I let God take over was my mind. My anxiety was very bad.

My thoughts wouldn't allow for me to get through regular activities. It got to a point where I could barely stand my thoughts. Sleeping was my only way to cope. After many months of many prayers and slow revelations, God took my anxiety away. Then after that it was dating,

God put it on my heart not to entertain any men for 6 months, and I realized SO much about my unhealthy dating habits. Within that time, I met other young black adults who showed me that celibacy is realistic and best for me and in March of 2016, I vowed to practice celibacy. Since then, I go about dating in a much more healthy manner and I know when to stay or leave. Next I gave God my money. Ironically, God placed it on my heart that in order to get more money – I have to leave a lucrative world of sales and get a job in advertising. I was never happy in sales, and I knew what I wanted to do but it took a mentor saying it which told me it was Godsent. I applied for to an ad agency in Cleveland, felt so much ease in the interview and was offered the job.

I know that was solely God. I've never been very good with money, but God has allowed me to nearly cut my rent in half and refinance my car. Plus, he laid a savings plan on my heart that is going very well. Through prayer, God also told me to invest in myself and seek out positivity. I began a podcast, a website, traveled and vowed to be a consistent reader. Before I began pursuing God, all of these things would have never hapened but God gave me confirmation that I am living in my purpose. I believe God brought me to Cleveland to remove me from all distractions and finally give myself time to pursue him. I'm excited to see what else He puts on my heart next!

Its scary a thing to give God the green light to lead your life. For 22 years, I was doing it myself. But looking back, that explains why my life was either very high or very low. I wouldn't allow God to steer and grab a hold of my heart and teach me joy, discernment and obedience. People always say to me "you seem so much happier" and I know they are seeing the God that I am pursuing within me.

Chapter 2:

Holding on to My College Days

"Do not be anxious about anything, but in every situation, by prayer and petition, with thanksgiving, present your requests to God. And the peace of God, which transcends all understanding, will guard your hearts and your minds in Christ Jesus."
-Philippians 4:6-7

The problem started while I was still in school. I was so worried about what life after graduation would be like. I knew I would miss my roommates, would not have my own space anymore due to me moving back home (which was a blessing, do not get me wrong), and I had not secured a job! It felt like all of my peers had everything lined up while I was wandering aimlessly through the wilderness.

I can vividly remember the day I moved into my college dorm my freshman year and it felt like it was just yesterday. As young 18-year-olds, my room mate, Etinosa and I were so excited for the new adventure and experiences college would bring. We explored campus together and took every opportunity by the horns. The years after that were full of ups and downs including a tough breakup, fun new experiences, the start of my personal brand, and so much more. Where did the four long years go so quickly?

I knew there would be no more roomie nights with my roommates, and that we would be separated by hundreds of miles and it stressed me out everytime we talked about it! Anxiety began to consume me and fear of the unknown constantly worried me as I tried to figure out what my life would look like outside of my current reality.

I grew so much in college and learned so much about myself that I couldn't rememember what life beforehand was like. College was the place where I fell in love with myself and had my dreams and goals nurtured. I wondered if it would stay the same outside of these imaginary college walls.

As I reflected on what it would mean to graduate and achieve such an amazing accomplishment, I realized there would be no more random late night trips to Wal-Mart, impromptu movie nights, or busting into Taylor's room when I got bored or just needed a hug. In College, the majority of my close friends were only a few minutes away from me but I knew that was all getting ready to change and I could hardly bare the thought of it. My college friends are originally from Chicago, St. Louis, New Orleans, and Kansas City and would be heading back home after graduation so I knew seeing them on a frequent basis would be next to impossible once we graduated!

If you have seen my college vlogs on youtube.com/SimplyDrea, you know how much fun my friends and I had. They could make me laugh just by doing the weirdest things and we bonded over some of the hardest moments we've ever had. For some odd reason, I knew I would miss even our late night study sessions in the library when we could barely keep our eyes open while munching on the most unhealthy snacks we could find in the student center. Those moments were so simple, yet they meant the world to me and I was sure I would miss it more than anything.

Yes, I know we have all different types of technology to stay in touch, but it was evident that it would not be the same. Sometimes you need a hug when you have just had your heartbroken or feel defeated by what life is throwing at you. Or occasionally you want someone to go on a random adventure with, and Taylor, my college roommate and adventure buddy, was now going to be over 950 miles away from me. College in general was such an amazing experience, I recognized I would miss it and I was 1000% right.

On graduation day, my family came rolling up to their hotel in a giant white van they rented because there were too many of them to fit in any other car. They came to celebrate my graduation with me and see Mizzou's beautiful campus where I had been for the past 4 years. Like always, I was so excited to see my family. Yet when I saw them, it hit me like a ton of bricks that my time in college, as a Mizzou Tiger, was officially coming to an end. I was torn with emotions. I was sad, extremely excited, proud of myself and terrified of what was next.

Looking back, I can now see that the reason I was so worried was simply because I was afraid of the unexpected. Instead of worrying about what was next, I wish I would have gotten on my knees and asked God for guidance and courage as I left what had become my second home.

I also realized that though I had the time of my life in college I noted something extremely troubling. I could count on both hands how many times I had been to church during the last four years in college. I did not put my faith first or anywhere close and when I look back, I can see the effects of it. No wonder I was so worried and stressed out, I was leaning on my own strength and trusting my own understanding rather than my Heavenly Father's. I claimed the drivers seat and put God in the trunk, only opening it when I was in trouble or at my lowest. The entire time, He should have been in the position that I had taken for myself.

When it comes to my faith, college was not one of my proudest moments. I had fun but with this, I had distanced myself from God more than ever before. The scariest mindset to be in, is to think that we can make it without Him... and that is exactly where I was. I used Sundays specifically for homework and study days without a thought of observing the Sabbath as He tells us to. I was so busy that I know I didn't make time to feed my spirit with His word and guidance. I became hard and defensive toward so many things and forgot all about what He called me to do! Going out, having fun with my friends and line sisters, and even school had become priority over my faith.

It was time to be pulled out of my comfort zone and back into the arms of God and that is slowly what happened as I headed back home to Dallas, Texas! If I would have been closer to the navigator of my life, maybe He would have told me not to worry about my career and that what is ahead is something that I could never even imagine, if I just stay patient! What happens next truly taught me to lean on God for guidance during my transition and for the rest of my life knowing that He will surely direct my path as He promised me.

As Proverbs 3:6, states, "Trust in the Lord with all your heart and lean not on your own understanding; In all your ways submit to Him, and He will make your paths straight. (NIV)

Theresa- 22 years old, University of Central Florida (@mrsladyyt_)

On December 25, 2011 I received the greatest news in the world, "Congratulations! We are pleased to extend an offer of acceptance to Howard University…".

Everything was right on track for my plan of life, you see, my mother attended Howard University and graduated Class of '84. Every day I passed the photo of my Mother and my grandmother standing on the steps of Douglass Hall, holding her degree on her graduation day. It soon turned into my goal to recreate that picture with me and my mother standing on the steps of Douglass Hall holding my degree from Howard University.

During my junior year at Howard, my childhood best friend begged me to apply for the Disney College Program. I had always dreamed of working at Disney but never really planned on applying for any jobs there and especially had no intentions of doing the college internship program. I applied with no intentions of getting in or even going if I was to be accepted into the program. At least I thought that until I got an acceptance email and I found out where I had been placed. It took me less than 30 seconds to whip out my wallet and pay the $300 non-refundable enrollment fee that locked my position in the program. Not to mention, I was just got engaged to my Brazilian husband, so I was thinking to live in Florida would be perfect considering the large Brazilian community they have there. I was completely over the moon to go work at Disney I decided to milk the whole thing. I wanted to move to Florida and transition my whole life down there and I wasn't going to wait until graduation, I had to go now. The week after I was accepted in to the program I already had my transfer application sent to the University of Central Florida and had put a deposit down on an apartment there in Orlando on Disney property.

A WEEK before my start day, with my boxes packed, my mother had to shake me saying I was making a mistake and I had an unrealistic view on how I would be able to support myself, or even just figure out life. I stepped back and realized I was marching to the beat of my own drum; I hadn't consulted God about my decision at all. Soon, my whole plan just came crumbling down, I was no longer a student at Howard, I was out a good $600 behind apartment fees and deposits, and I was confused on my next step.

This whole lesson of leaning on my own understanding was an eye-opening one. God used my mom to halt the process with Him knowing exactly how that would have ended: divorced, broke, and ashamed. Now, I work for the most amazing nonprofit organization that serves orphaned and vulnerable children. My husband and I are happier than ever before and I am almost finished my degree through The University of Central Florida.

God's hand has truly been on my life and I have learned to ask for His guidance through every decision. I've submitted my life to God, trusting and knowing that He will guide me in the direction of my future!

Chapter 3:

Is There a Class on Adulting?

"Come to me, all you who are weary and burdened, and I will give you rest." – Matthew 11:28

My first job out of college was nothing less than horrible. The job was sold to me as an intriguing marketing position where I would be managing multiple projects and creating marketing campaigns for B2B companies. I was told that my communication degree would be very useful and that I would consult with my customers via phone but I would only be on the phone for two hours out of the day. Marketing was the area I wanted to be in so I was elated to land a job in my field, especially only being one month out of college!

Very quickly my excitement came to a screeching halt. After a few days of training I realized that it was a telemarketer/sales job where I sat on the phone all day and annoyed countless people with hundreds of unwanted calls a week. You know when you get random numbers calling your phone about something you've never signed up for? Yea, well, that probably me on the other end of the call lol. I'm not saying anything is wrong with sales positions; it just was not what I signed up for. The job description was extremely deceptive and I knew that I was lied to. The products we sold were worthless and extremely overpriced for the amount of nothing they were getting. I can not even begin to count the number of times I was hung up on, yelled at for continuously getting calls from our company, or cussed out because they did not want to talk to us. Getting such negative feedback on such a consistent basis can really mess up your morale, especially if you never had a desire to do a position such as that one in the first place!

On top of all of that, we were micromanaged, had our phone minutes monitored and our calls constantly listened to and critiqued. They treated us as though we were kindergarteners and looked down on every action we took. I was beyond frustrated, considering I had never worked for a company that did not trust me and flat out lied to me about my job description. The lack of transparency seemed to be a constant discussion amongst coworkers and was one of my biggest concerns. Also, it was routine for the company to fire around 30 people at a time without even a days notice on occasional Fridays. Employees were always on edge on due to the uncertainty of what the next Friday would bring and how they would feed their kids or pay bills if they were grouped in the spontaneous firings.

From the outside, the job seemed amazing and the company looked like it was a fun atmosphere: an upbeat, young environment where employees worked hard and played hard. But this was not the case. It was a call center, point, blank, period and that is not what was communicated to me in the interview or job description. It paid well but I knew it was not for me and one day, after the longest three months of my life, I could not take it anymore. I wrote my resignation letter, put in my two weeks notice and I was out the door! It was such a horrible job and unlike anything I have ever been a part of. As my first career move after college, it was truly one that I will never forget.

On top of the stress of that job, I became more critical of myself and my situation due to looking at others lives through the lens of social media. Social media can be such an amazing way to keep up with friends both new and old! It can also be 'free' advertising for your brand or business, plus tons of other benefits. But the downside of social media is that it can make it so easy to compare your stage in life to someone else's portrayed reality! You see some of your graduating classmates have such glamorous jobs, cars, relationships, or friends and you look at yourself and question what happened, at least that is what happened to me. Everything seemed to be going perfectly for the majority of my graduating class and I begin to doubt myself because I wondered where I went wrong.

Just remember, things are not always as they seem. People only post what looks good and portrays them in a positive light. You must keep in mind that though it may look like Sally has it all together, there is a high chance that she is having her struggles too, just behind the scenes. Heed my warning and know that your first job right out of college may not be your dream job and that is TOTALLY OKAY! This doesn't mean you're stuck or will always be in the same position either. A lot of times you just have to start somewhere. It can be a very scary and tough time, trust me I know and I've lived it; especially coming out of college and trying to adjust to 'adult life' while forcing yourself up each morning to go to a job that drains every bit of happiness out of you.

I had to learn the hard way that experience in the work field trumps a college degree. You have to put your time in and work your way up. Pick a company that you can see yourself growing in and work your way up from there.

You may not start out where you want,

but as long as you get your foot in the door and have a game plan, you will get there. Entry level positions could include customer service representative, executive assistant, sales consultant, secretary, or administrative assistant. In any position you are in, plan to excel! Show your skills and go above and beyond your duties. It may seem as though no one notices, but they do!

Looking back to when I was in college, I wish I had been more proactive with my job search. I felt so bogged down with school and the many hats I wore that I failed to think about my post-grad life and what that even meant. As president of The Intercollegiate Communication Organization of Mizzou, a Nationally Certified Fitness Instructor at our Student Rec Center (#1 in the country by the way: Fun fact), and an active member of my sorority, Alpha Kappa Alpha, I had a lot to deal with at once. Not to mention I also owned and operated my still up and running Lifestyle and Beauty blog (SimplyDrea.com) and managed my YouTube channel. I had little down time, or so I thought, to actively search for positions in the fields I wanted to be in. Not being proactive when it came to my job search was a huge mistake on my part but I'm here to now warn you against that.

If you are still in college, my advice for you:

Set a specific time during your semester prior to graduation to search for positions, contact people from old internships, and reach out to professionals you know. Do not wait until you walk across the stage to start looking! If you wind up like me, know that everything will still be okay, it just may be a little harder. I was so nervous about the future I failed to plan for it, like that would prevent it from coming. So please, please be proactive and search months before your graduation day!

It took me a while to even realize it but my problem did not start after graduation it started months before. My lack of planning, overwhelming feeling of doubt, and avoiding the inevitable were my biggest mistakes. But hey, once we make those mistakes we have an opportunity to grow from them. Either way, no matter the route you take, it is going to be a huge adjustment that you will have to eventually get used to. Once you do, you will be just fine!

Jen - 35 years old, Loving Wife, Mom, and Professional
@wejwalk4life

Well....I thought it would be easy! Lol....not:) I graduated with a BA of Sociology with not a clue what to really do with it. My parents really thought I was on a mission to do such amazing, save the world type things! In reality, I was petrified! Didn't want to seem like a failure with a degree. I carried on though....just going with the flow and with whatever I thought would look good to my parents. For a good while I did great, self sufficient, had great friends, my independence ....then love struck (boyfriend then and husband now) and I moved in with my parents to be in closer proximity to him.

I told my parents it would be an awesome money saver and would help me pay off my student loans faster. LIES! Still got student loans! Shortly after moving back home, it hit me, driving to my hated job at the time......mood changed drastically and I was in awe at how down I felt about my life at that time. Not happy at my job, no major traveling done and I felt I hadn't accomplished anything with my degree. I felt terrible and didn't know where to start with my thoughts on how to resolve. I just knew I couldn't give up and couldn't wait for a handout! Eventually,

God revealed a desire of determination in myself that I otherwise would not have known existed. I pushed through and resourced through what God had provided to me. Step one: I moved out of my parent's house since I moved in for the wrong reason and created a fresh start. I realized quickly that I was not alone and that what I was going through, someone else was going through too or had already been through my same experiences. Situations and emotions will work it's way out for God's purpose, was what I kept hearing in various ways. Hindsight.... the uncomfortable part was God stretching and preparing me......hard to believe at the time but it made sense!!

I'm so grateful for those constant reminders especially from those you know care genuinely about your well-being. Besides, who's really kept track of how many stumbles I took...take! Ha :) It took a little while but things started to take shape and situations didn't look quite as dreary! My expectations for life after college were not of my coolest or ideal situation but it happened according to the plan He set for me! For that I'm grateful and would encourage any college graduate to embrace the time given to figure things out and don't be so quick to judge your situation as a fail.

Life lesson: Your degrees don't determine your path, it just assists with your ideas! Leaders are never afraid to fail!! Remember your youth and be open to stumbles.....God turns them into your stepping stones toward success, if you trust in His will.

Chapter 4:

The Waiting Season

"So do not fear, for I am with you; do not be dismayed, for I am your God. I will strengthen you and help you; I will uphold you with my righteous right hand." – Isaiah 41:10

After leaving that awful job, I was once again, in a lull. I had no job and was pursuing YouTube and blogging "full-time" at least that is what I would say when people asked me! That simply meant I was working on my channel and blog but that did not mean that I had enough revenue flowing in to keep the lights on! I threw myself completely into blogging and YouTube and would head to a different library or Starbucks everyday to get work done.

Soon, one month later in fact, I realized that God was not necessarily calling me to be a full time content creator at that moment. I could knew it because I did not have peace about it. I would sit in the library trying to go full throttle for my channel and brand but something was off. Once I finally realized this, I threw in the towel and began searching for jobs. As I started looking, the doubt began to sink in, again.

Everywhere I looked there seemed to be positions that looked just as horrible as my last job. I knew I never wanted to be in a position like that again, but it seemed like that was all that was out there. I was getting so discouraged and questioned if I would ever find a company whose mission I believed in and wanted to give hours of my time to its cause! I just knew that 40+ hours a week was too much to not either enjoy what I'm doing or work towards a purpose I believed in. At that point,

I had a mini melt down!

As I continued to look for jobs, I knew what I wanted to do, I just did not know how to get there. Have you ever felt like a ship that has lost its sail or a fish that cannot find its way to water? That was me, lost with no idea which direction to head which was starting to become a familiar feeling for me.

One of the best, yet hardest, decisions I made was to begin to ask around for help. A lot of times we feel as though we know it all and have everything figured out when all we have to do is ask for advice. So, I swallowed my pride and began to ask for help from various people and resources. I tapped into my family and church members first.

My Aunt Gloria works in HR and had a lot of connections in my area but I was so set on figuring it out myself that I did not think to reach out to her. She would ask me what my plan was in terms of my job search and every time she asked I would get defensive because honestly, I felt inadequate. I was struggling to find any positions worth pursuing which was making me question my skills and talents. Every job opening that looked interesting seemed to require 90+ years of experience or an inside connection that I did not have. As I continued searching, I would get more discouraged which caused me to become extremely sensitive whenever I was asked about it.

After the battle of feeling incompetent and dealing with my pride was over, I was able to start with a clean slate and open mind. I reached out to my Aunt Gloria again and she was able to connect me to Crysta, who is a family friend of ours. She works at a company I was interested in and talked with me about what I was looking for. We fleshed out where I wanted to go career wise and different positions within her company that could help get me there. She then had me fill out an application and she was able to connect me to others within her company. I am so grateful for the advice she shared with me and having someone on the inside to pass my application to the people who needed it.

Advice: Use your connections; It's all in who you know!

Soon after submitting the application, I got a call from the company asking me to come interview for their customer service representative position. I was so excited to finally start the interview process but of course, that came with a few nerves. I finally felt like the ball was rolling and I was going to be out of my jobless misery soon.

The interview day came, and after talking to myself in my car the whole way there, I felt ready. I walked into a huge building in my business professional suit and heels, trying to compose myself and calm my nerves. I was interviewing with a big and very well established company and that alone made me anxious! When my name was called to go back to where the interview was taking place my stomach literally turned flips. The interview was tough and straightforward. I had prepared for it but realized afterward that my preparation was not enough. Walking out I knew that it wasn't my best but was hoping that they thought differently. I was told it would be approximately two weeks until I heard back so in the meantime, I kept my fingers crossed and kept looking for different job opportunities.

I reached out to various people for advice on what they did and how they overcame this transition from college to the working world. I got in contact with some of my sorority sisters who were older than me, my previous graduate advisor from an organization I was president of, and older friends and family. This was hands down one of the best things I did because for the first time I realized I was not the only one who struggled during this unknown time! No my misery does not like company but it is comforting to know you aren't the only one who is facing a particular storm.

After speaking with each of them for hours, I discovered that they all realized there was no straight path to success. They all thought it was going to be different than how it actually turned out. One went to grad school because she didn't know what her other options were, one moved across the country to find out that she would soon hate her job, and one had just ended a relationship and did not know what her next step was. After hearing their different stories and struggles, I started to realize that I was not alone and that it would all work out. Slowly, it all started clicking. Speaking to old friends and family was a huge game changer. They assured me everything would be just fine and though I had a degree, I may have to start out in a position and work my way up or take a different path I did not expect to take.

My old college advisor, Megan, told me her story about choosing to go to grad school and tossing around what her next step would be as well. This planted the grad school idea in my head that I started thinking could be a strong possibility because I always heard, 'If you don't know what else to do, go back to school.' The problem with grad school was that it was extremely expensive and I was not completely sure it was the step I should take but despite this, I started looking around at different schools and became really interested in the University of North Texas (UNT).

After doing a good amount of research, I came to the conclusion a MBA in Marketing would be the best route for me. I then contacted the lead from the UNT Business department to set up a meeting. I also set up a tour of the campus and all of its facilities. When the day came to tour the school, I had already convinced myself that this would be my next move so I was becoming hopeful. But I had to stop myself and consider not only the costs but also my true motive behind wanting to go.

Now, I'm not saying that this was my only motivation behind wanting to go to grad school, but as a young single woman, I thought it would also be a great place to meet a guy. Something I was told is that college is a great place to meet your husband so the fact that I came out of undergrad completely single had gotten to me, if I'm being honest. Once I thought the decision through and went over how much money I had left in my trust fund, I recognized I was trying to go to grad school for all the wrong reasons. If God was not leading me to do it at that time, it could cause problems down the road. Though getting my masters was still in the back of my mind I knew it was not the right time, so I was forced to go back to the drawing board. I went back to my job search and began submitting applications once again.

Reaching out to others was working in my

favor so I also reached out to the praise dance team at my church for advice. I'd danced with them for years and knew they were older than me and had more experience in the working world. As we sat around chatting about life after practice, I brought up my need for a job and my concern about not wanting to get involved with another job like the previous one. As we stood outside by our cars, they began giving me options and different job titles to explore. They told me to look in the categories of customer service positions, customer relations, retail management, and executive assistants positions. Jen and Cineada, members of the praise dance team, told me administrative and executive assistant positions were great starting places. They knew a lot of people who got their foot in the door through those types of positions. Though I was not completely ecstatic at the thought of those positions, I decided to look into them. I had nothing to lose and you have to start somewhere, right?

A few nights later, my line sister, Callie and I had our routine phone conversation and I brought to her my concern about my job search.

She expressed to me that when she graduated two years prior she had the same struggles. She felt like over time, she slowly found her way and ended up in a position she loved. She recommended that I also apply for a similar position as hers with the company she was with and that she would recommend me so I ran after the opportunity!

While sitting at my kitchen table with my laptop and notebook, I took a little bit of everyone's advice and applied to executive assistant roles, retail manager positions, and customer service reps. That day the company Crista works for called and told me they decided to go with other candidates... my heart dropped. Though I was applying for other positions, I really wanted to get my foot in the door at that company. I had my hopes up for that opportunity and just thought that somehow, though I didn't think my interview went well, I'd get the position. After getting myself together and picking up my sad spirit. I got my head back in the game. I decided I wasn't going to let my situation define me or steal my joy. The call from that company made me look for jobs even more diligently. That same day I applied to so many jobs of various different positions and I was exhausted. My plan was to keep doing this until I got a job so I was applying to about 8 companies a day.

Soon enough, on a Friday afternoon, my efforts began paying off and companies started calling me to schedule interviews. I lined up interviews for the entire next week and needed to start preparing.

When Monday came around, I was ready. Of course, I was really nervous but I made sure I was prayed up and prepared. As I went into the different interviews I realized a lot of them were just like my old job, I just had not been able to sift them out using the Internet like I thought I could. Tuesday rolled around and I had two interviews, one in the morning and one in the afternoon. The first one was with the company my sister Callie worked for and the second was an interview with a marketing company. The interview was scheduled for three o'clock and of course I was on time, meaning 12 minutes early. I walked into the office doors, after getting off the elevator, and it was weirdly quiet and stuffy. There was no creative touch to the office and the office had no paintings or sayings on the walls and the overall vibe was off compared to what I read online. I sat down, after giving the receptionist my name and realized that three other people were sitting there with me. I wondered if it was a group interview or if they were just really early as well. After talking to the interviewer, I realized this was not like my old job... it was worse.

They wanted me to stand in a Home improvement store and sell kitchen upgrades to people as they walked out. No thank you! The interview lasted about 13 minutes and as I walked to my car, I hung my head in defeat. Not because the interview did not go well, but because I knew it was another job with no purpose or meaning behind it and it was looking like I was going to just settle for one of those opportunties. I tried to let go of the disappointment and focus on the two interviews I had the next day that I needed to shine in but it was almost impossible. Doubt began to creep into my mind on whether I would ever find the job for me! I had seriously begun to question whether my degree was even worth it.

Why spend all that money and time if I can't get a stable, fun, and reliable job after college?

Wednesday came and I was nervous, but ready for the interview as a retail manager. This was the position my line sister, Callie suggested I apply for. But about an hour before the interview, I received a call from another organization interested in my resume. The Vice President of Human Resources from one of the companies I applied to wanted to set up an interview that week. Though I already blocked off that Friday because it was my 23rd birthday, I agreed to interview at nine o'clock on Friday. There was no other time open and I knew that I honestly wasn't doing anything that morning anyway so I agreed to be there. This was one of companies I was extremely interested in but I had to switch gears back to the interview that I had now in 45 minutes.

It was finally time to go in. So, I walked into the store, after taking a few deep breaths to get rid of the nerves, I was immediately greeted with smiles and acknowledgments from the employees. The manager asked me basic interview questions such as why I wanted to work there and what I could add to the team. She explained in depth what the position would look like. As the interview was coming to an end, the manager said they really liked me and knew I would be a great fit to the team. She then followed up and asked me when I could let them know of a decision. The interview went amazing so, in my head, this opportunity excelled to the top of my list, which wasn't very long. Knowing that I had another interview that I felt led to go to before making a decision, I told the manager I would let her know my decision by Friday at 1:30 pm. I was so excited because I finally had an offer I was interested in!

That night, my Aunt Gloria, my friend Tati, and I went to Bible study at our church. Though I had different opportunities coming about, I had convinced myself not to get my hopes up quite yet. As I sat in the sanctuary listening to the worship music and trying to keep my mind from wandering, God spoke to me very clearly. He said, "Humble yourself and trust me."

This startled me because it was so loud

and was one of the clearest messages I had
ever heard from Him. I had no idea what He
meant or what He was implying so I asked Him,
"God, what do you mean and can I get some
clarification?" I did not receive an immediate
answer so, though I was confused, I waited,
keeping what He said in the back of my mind,
hoping that He would soon reveal the meaning
behind what He spoke to me.

Janine– 25 years old, Magazine Journalist/ Strategic Communication Specialist

(@ janine_patrice)

Between graduating with my Bachelor of Journalism degree in 2014 and now, I've experienced the most growth and set backs than any other point in my life. I accepted an internship with a magazine the following fall and later worked as a full-time résumé writer due to the difficulties in finding career opportunities in the magazine industry within the St. Louis, MO region.

At this point, I felt as though I was stuck and began questioning my passions and abilities; should I have studied in a STEM-related field? Why could I not have chosen a career path that would have more opportunities to get my foot in the door? I began to feel hopeless about my next steps and it seemed as though my future wouldn't include me having a job that I loved in the industry that I was most passionate about. My parents encouraged me to always go for what I want in life and not necessarily what may make more money because that does not always lead to happiness.

In the summer of 2015, I began looking into graduate school programs to expand my knowledge in the media industry. Once I got accepted into Maryville University's Strategic Communication and Leadership program, I was hopeful that obtaining my masters would be a way for me to be even more marketable in the communications industry. I successfully completed the program and am currently interviewing with companies all over the country.

The most important lesson I have learned in this part of my life is that patience is key and worrying about the future does nothing to help your growth. Taking action in the direction that you wish to go and waiting for your life to unfold as you take these steps will guide you in the right direction. Always keep your faith strong and know that what is for you will never pass you.

Chapter 5:

My Blessing in Disguise

"For I know the plans I have for you," declares the Lord, "plans to prosper you and not to harm you, plans to give you hope and a future." – Jeremiah 29:11

As I continued my job search, every now and then, the message God spoke to me that Wednesday night would come back to me. But I did not harp on it too much with hopes that He would show me exactly what He meant in His perfect timing without me going to search for the explanation myself.

Thursday night, I began to prepare for both

my birthday festivities and my last interview of
the week. While researching the organization, I
came across a video on their website. Curious and
hoping to get more insight on the organization,
I watched the video and within 20 seconds tears
were rolling down my face. The video captured the
mission of the organization and though I did not
quite understand what was going on, I knew that
God's hand was in it, which I absolutely loved! The
video seemed to feature a mission trip: Americans
of all ages were holding the cutest African children
in there arms, instilling the word of God into them,
teaching them God loves them, and that they are
beautifully and wonderfully made in God's image.
I got emotional watching one of the participants
wave goodbye to the children, riding away in a
bus, with tears streaming down their faces. After
watching this, I needed to know more! I looked
into every aspect of the organization because this
felt like something I would truly love.

      Friday morning finally came and it was time
for me to gather my things, look over my notes one
last time and begin to head to the office.
Once I arrived, my nerves started up as I had
expected they would but I repeated Philippians

4:13 to myself over and over again, said a prayer, and walked in confidently. The overall interview was one of the most comfortable interviews I had ever been in. Though it was structured in the same way every other interview was, something felt different.

There was a sense of peace that I had never quite felt in a situation like this. At the end of the interview, I was asked to take a Style of Influence assessment, a quiz that assesses your working habits and personality to understand how they would line up with others at the organization. I was told I wouldn't hear back about the position until the middle or end of the next week. But I quickly remembered I had another job offer, the job that Callie referred me to, that I needed to make a decision about by noon. After expressing my concern to the interviewer, who is the Vice President of Human Resources at the organization, she attempted to contact Holly, who would be my manager should I get the position. She expressed that she really wanted me to talk with Holly but the only thing was she wouldn't be in the office until ten o'clock. So even though it was my birthday I decided to wait, I honestly had no real plans that morning and because I was so interested in the position, I wanted to move the process along as quick as possible.

When Holly came in, she flashed an instant smile and sat down right next to me. We talked about different aspects of what the job would entail and what she needed in an executive assistant. I could see she was a very busy woman but I also sensed how sweet of a person she was. She asked me why I felt led to work to work there and what the connection was between the organization and myself so I told her my story (which you will hear about in detail in my upcoming book, so stay tuned).

As I talked, she began to cry and said, "Wow, I feel blessed to even know you and sit with you." About 35 minutes later, the second interview was over and Holly showed me around the office, introduced me to the President/CEO, other staff members, and handed me a stack of informational materials about the organization. I felt as though I had it in the bag but as I was leaving Holly told me she would be following up but "It was all in God's hands." This comment shook me and made me take back my previous thought of, "I got this." I walked out of the office and said a prayer, "If this is in Your will Lord, PLEASE let me get this job! It seems like the perfect position but I place this completely in Your hands and trust that You know what is best for me."

All I could think about as I was driving home was how the interview went and how badly I wanted the position; but I tried to let it go and completely give it to God to work out. When I got home, I told my aunt and uncle how it went and they assured me they would say a prayer. My aunt Gloria who works in HR, gave me advice that if anyone relating to a job calls me to follow up, let them leave a voicemail so that you make sure you get all the info and can replay it if necessary. But it was three o'clock on a Friday so I was sure I wouldn't hear from them that day. And since it was my birthday, I went upstairs to my room to get ready for my birthday dinner and night out with my girls. As I was preparing to do my makeup and figure out my outfit for the night, I checked my phone and saw I had a missed call. It was the VP of HR calling me to let me know they had made a decision.

They wanted to bring me on board! Only four hours after my interview ended, they had made a decision and I was ecstatic!

I ran downstairs as fast as I could to tell my aunt and uncle the news, they were surprised and equally excited. I asked for their thoughts on what exactly I should do in terms of responding. They had differing opinions, my aunt said the professional thing to do is wait 24 hours before responding while my uncle said, "Go for it!" Listening to my Aunt's advice, I gave the VP of HR a call back and let her know that I appreciated the offer but would like to take some time to think about it and get back with her on Monday.

Right when I hung up the phone, I felt uncomfortable. It was weird; I was not at peace at all with the decision to wait to accept the position even though I KNEW I wanted to take it. I ran back downstairs and talked with my aunt and uncle again and they had the same stances as before. My fear was that they would interview or consider someone else before I could accept it and that I would pass it up. Eventually, after going back and forth in my mind, I asked my aunt her thoughts one last time, "If you want it, and since it's your birthday, go ahead and call her back so you aren't worrying about it tonight and over the weekend." Within 20 minutes of telling her that I would let her know my decision on Monday, I called back and accepted the position. She was so elated and welcomed me to the team and I was grinning ear-to-ear knowing that I was now employed after what felt like an eternity!

It was then that God showed me what He meant when He told me to trust Him and humble myself. He meant just that: trust Him that He has it all under control and to humble myself to be someone's assistant and serve His precious children in Africa.

Alexa– 23 years old, Future Educator & Group Fitness Instructor (@ alexakpace)

What I expected out of post grad life was almost like a fairytale in regards to reality: instead of the luxurious beginning of my career and the start of the exciting "real world" I longed for, I ended up with the type of sales job I intended to steer clear from, and the loneliness that moving back to your hometown can bring. Don't get me wrong, I felt extremely blessed to have a well-paying job lined up out of school, and that I was fortunate enough to move back home to save money. However, I think that most new college grads have a vision of what their life will turn into once they walk across the stage with their flashy new diploma, and rarely do those visions occur instantly.

In the year proceeding graduation, I wish-washed back and forth between what I really wanted to do with my life—none of the options on the table having a direct correlation to my college degree buy the way—and I found myself extremely lost. My college friends were scattered around the country, and childhood ones alike. Although I was back in the place I began, I felt like I had to start over again. It was like my life ended at college and was no longer fun anymore. I no longer had the time for pursuing hobbies with my long work hours, and it was a struggle keeping in touch with friends through social media or by phone.

It was not until the fall, when school started up for students again, that I realized that though I was living in the "real world," I was still young and had the opportunity to pursue my dreams, whatever they may be. I began applying for graduate school and created a plan for myself. I would no longer live the mundane, day-to-day routine I found my co- workers stuck in. I needed to break out and do something.

About a year to date of my graduation day, I find

myself back in school again. Funny how things come full circle, but I am grateful that it did not take me too long to pursue what I truly want. I now have a clear view of my future, both in the short term and long term; however, I am now aware that it is okay to not be the highly successful career woman right away. It takes time, patience and faith that the path meant for you will present itself when necessary.

Chapter 6:

Here God, Take Back This Wheel

"Humble yourselves, therefore, under God's mighty hand, that He may lift you up in due time." – 1 Peter 5:6

When I started my new job, I was welcomed with open arms and everyone expressed how excited they were for me to be there. Holly wrote me the cutest letter, that is still propped up in front of my computer. As time passed and I got more comfortable with the position and my coworkers; I thought more and more about how thankful I was to be able to call this amazing organization my work home. Everyday, Holly reminded me of how thankful she was for me. Though it is not needed, it is always amazing to feel loved and appreciated at your job.

Around the middle of December, we were sitting in Holly's office discussing everything that needed to be done before she went to Zambia, when she had an idea. Holly asked me if I had any plans for the two week period she would be in Zambia, catching onto what she was thinking I smiled and said no. Next thing I knew, only two months after working for the organization, I was on a plane heading to Africa to serve the orphaned and vulnerable children of Zambia. I traveled through both London, England and Johannesburg, South Africa to get to Zambia. Since I was a little girl, I always wanted to someday travel to Africa and look at what God had lined up. Not only was I getting the opportunity to travel to the place I had always desired to go but I was also getting to do God's work while there!

Sitting on the plane, I remembered Him saying, "Trust me and humble yourself," and it became more evident why He said it. I needed to remove myself out of the equation for Him to work in the way He wanted to. I was heading half way across the world with the job God was preparing me for. Is God not amazing?! I was getting the chance to go to the motherland and pour God's love into His children, whose situations were similar to mine, parentless and vulnerable. Losing my parents at the age of 13, was a pain beyond words, but I never would have imagined at the time that my life would somehow come full circle!

Being in Zambia was an unforgettable experience. It definitely had its ups and downs but God was surely present and I could see Him in the eyes of the precious children. I know for a fact, that I would not have been in my situation if I had not walked in obedience and listened to the words He spoke to me that Wednesday night in Bible Study.

With this position not only did God open a door for me to travel to a country in Africa but I also got the chance to go to Google Headquarters in Mountain View, California with Holly and our CFO. We had the privilege of hosting a food-packing event where our company partnered with Google to provide over 250,000 meals for our children in Zambia. Google Headquarters was everything you see in movies and online and they welcomed us with open arms. The experience was unmatched and I am so grateful that we had the opportunity to go.

Throughout my time in California with our organization, the words "Trust me and humble yourself," continued to circle back in my mind as God unpacked the meaning behind His message. God continues to show His love and kindness as I walk in obedience with Him and stay aligned with His guidance!

Now, I say all of this not to say that I have made it out or figured it all out by any means. Adulting is still a struggle! I say this and tell you my experience to let you know it is all unpredictable to us yet totally in God's hands and that it WILL get better.

Coming out of college I had no idea which direction to go and felt lost in the 'adult world'. I had to understand that, if we knew it all or had it all figured out we may get prideful and think we can do it without Him, which is, like I mentioned before, a dangerous space to be in. Though I love the organization I am with now, like every organization, there are highs and lows. No matter where my career takes me I have learned a serious lesson in trusting God and His plans.

The sharing of my story is simply to let you see that none of this journey has been in my control, the day I let go and turned my life completely over to my Heavenly Father, everything changed for the better. Life is a journey and it is your choice on whether or not you want to grab God's hand and let Him lead you. When I was living in pride and fighting against God's guidance I was so focused on what was next and I became stressed and worried. This was just one big transition in my young 23-year- old life and I am sure there will be plenty more. What I have learned from this transition is not to stress or worry about my future. I know that If I hand it all over to God, He will guide me in the direction to where I need to be.

During whatever transition you are in life, commit to yourself not to worry. Worry and faith cannot occupy the same space. We serve an all knowing, all powerful, loving and just God who will never leave us, even when we unknowingly try to push Him away. Now, this is not to be confused with just sitting around and waiting. Do your part and trust and believe that God will do the rest.

Here are a few things I hope can help you get you through any transition you are facing:

- **Pray**

  o God already knows your struggle and He wants you to confide in Him. Talk to God and ask for His guidance on your every move.

- **Leave it all in His hands**

  o No more worry, give your worry to Him and walk away from any doubt you may still have.

- **Confide in your Tribe**

  o Confide in faith driven friends around you for a shoulder to lean on and Godly advice. Don't have any? Join a small group at church.

- **Know your creator and His strength**

  o While you pass through your

transition, press into God when
times get hard. He is strongest
at our weakest.

- **Get Busy**

  o Ask God what it is that He wants
    you to do and run fearlessly
    towards it.

- **Know that it gets better**

  o It may be hard right now but use
    this time to grow in your walk
    with God and as an individual.
    Keep your head up and know that
    it will get better very soon!

- **Know you are not alone**

  o Most likely you are not the
    only one facing this storm.
    Connect and share your story to
    help others struggling through
    theirs on my platform www.
    SimplyDrea.com.

Jordan- 22 years old, Editor & Marketing Strategist (@Jordanallecea)

I remember starting my senior year of college, I felt amazing. I thought the whole world would be at my fingertips and I was so ready to start my life! That was all great until my job search really began, I constantly felt rejected. I wanted to live out my dream, I wanted to be a professional dancer.

I spent 15 years working toward this goal, I had a Bachelors of Fine Arts from the top dance school at a public university in the country! I knew it would be hard to accomplish, but I didn't quite understand how hard, I was told no audition after audition and it started to get to me. Self doubt creeped and I lost all confidence in myself, my talents, my body…everything. I got so tired of hearing no, I just gave up. I gave up on my dream.

Not only did no one want me in the dance world but my 'back up' plan was also falling through. My marketing degree was getting me nowhere. I went to interview after interview, I scoured the internet for good positions and all I ever heard back was, "we've decided to go with someone else." I felt defeated, rejected and honestly… worthless. I had spent four extremely hard (and expensive) years fighting to get my two degrees and after all that hard work nobody wanted me!

I couldn't bear the thought of coming back home without a job, so I took the first thing that was offered to me. It was not what I wanted to do, not in the industry I wanted to be in and the compensation did not match my education or experience level. But I was desperate, so I settled… and I was miserable.

I soon realized I couldn't do life without my Lord. I couldn't make decisions without Him, I couldn't apply to jobs without Him, I couldn't go to auditions without Him. My life is not my own and when I try to control everything, it all goes south.

I prayed and prayed and prayed and was blessed with a new job, at a company I had been trying to work with for years.

When I stopped to consult Him, ask Him questions, bring my problems to Him and simply talk to Him things started to turn around. I'm not saying things are perfect, because they most definitely are not; but things can only go up from here!

Chapter 7:

Teach Me to Trust You

"Cast all your anxiety on him because he cares for you" -1 Peter 5:7

God has truly shown Himself in this period of my life and I have never been closer to Him. Trusting God with my heart and my life has been one of the most rewarding things I have ever done, though at first it was terrifying. I have realized my life is not my own and if I walk in obedience, God will lead me to where He wants me which will be beyond what I could ever imagine. I have learned that in every aspect of my life to truly trust

Him and His timing. This means in my career, my purpose, and in my dating life (which, for me, is the hardest one). It is not easy to fully submit to God and His plan but it is the least stressful and most fulfilling way to go.

During this season of your life, know that God's got you and knows the best plan for your life but you must trust Him and walk in obedience!

During this season, I have specifically noticed more about God and myself because I have been more tuned into God working in my life than ever before.

Whenever He answers my prayers or blesses me with something, He does it in a way that I can't claim I had anything to do with it. It's done that way so I know, without a doubt, that it was all of Him and none of me. I had no part in the blessings or the connecting of dots aside from obedience. Opportunities have come about without any help from me, and people have stepped into my life that have been huge influences on this journey. My purpose has been noted and put into action, and all of this has come about simply due to God. The only thing I had to do was take my hands off the steering wheel and give God control over my situation and journey. I have seen God so clearly in this season and after experiencing Him like I do now, I never want to go back! He has used one of the most vulnerable and confused parts of my life to draw me in closer to Him. I have realized there is no need to worry when we serve a God who has already been in our tomorrow!

Coming out of college and into the 'real world' can be very frightening and beyond confusing. Though I have been a Christian for years, I was lost and had forgotten the need to place Jesus at the center of my life. I went back to my roots, which was trusting God even though I did not understand and it changed everything. This whole process is one heck of a journey and a very unexpected one at that, but if you change your perspective, it does not have to be all that bad. Look at this time as a new season of growth, in every aspect; a time to focus on finding your purpose and walking it out. It is not going to be perfect and it will not always be easy but that is totally okay and honestly can be the fun part of it all.

Even as I'm writing this book, my journey continues. I moved into a new apartment and soon after, anxiety started to creep back in. I was nervous about being alone and wondered if I had made the right decision to move out. On top of that, my good friend Jordan, also the editor of my book, moved all the way to Washington DC. for her job and it was hard on the both of us. We have been friends since Sophomore year of high school and I was so excited that after college we would have each other to hang out with back at home in Dallas. She is that friend I knew would keep me accountable but also was always down to have a good time. We were like two peas in a pod and went to basically every event and outing together! She is such an amazing friend and the fact that she would now be so far away, made me so sad. But then I realized it is not about me, it is all a part of our individual journeys we call life and it is okay.

I also, headed back to Zambia, Africa for a second time but this time traveled through Dubai, somewhere I had once only dreamed of going! Once in Zambia, I met so many more children in need of our love and attention. This trip was even better than the first one and these children have truly transformed my thinking and outlook on life. The fact that they are so happy with so little makes me see how much we truly take for granted in America. Their love and excitement to see us is so refreshing and to me, serving these amazing children in Lusaka, Zambia is the closest thing to heaven on Earth!

These constant changing events show us that our lives are continuous journeys and that is the point. The moment we realize that only God holds the timeline of our lives, the easier it gets! I never thought that post-grad life would be such an interesting time but nonetheless, it has been an experience. Growing up, paying bills, working, and being responsible with my time is definitely different than college. The months have literally flown by and I still cannot believe it has been a full year since I graduated from college! It feels like yesterday I was running around with my roommates having fun doing the simple things. I miss them like crazy but am so thankful for the memories and the amazing college experience I had!

I do not wish I could go back because this journey has been critical for my growth and the development of my purpose. Yes, I miss college but once you get a grasp on the unexpected, you will get use to adulting and begin to enjoy it. My advice to graduating seniors getting ready to take the leap into true adulthood is to let go! Let go of all expectations of how things are supposed to go. Grab hold of God's hand and let Him lead you, but get ready for an adventure. Get ready for the Journey Unexpected!

I want to hear from you!

If this book has helped you or you would like to share your story, email me at andrea@simplydrea.com! I'd love to hear from you!

On the next few pages, take some time to take any notes from the book or jot down some action items if you are getting ready to graduate from college or enter into a big life transition.

Andrea D. Boyd

Notes:

To - Do:

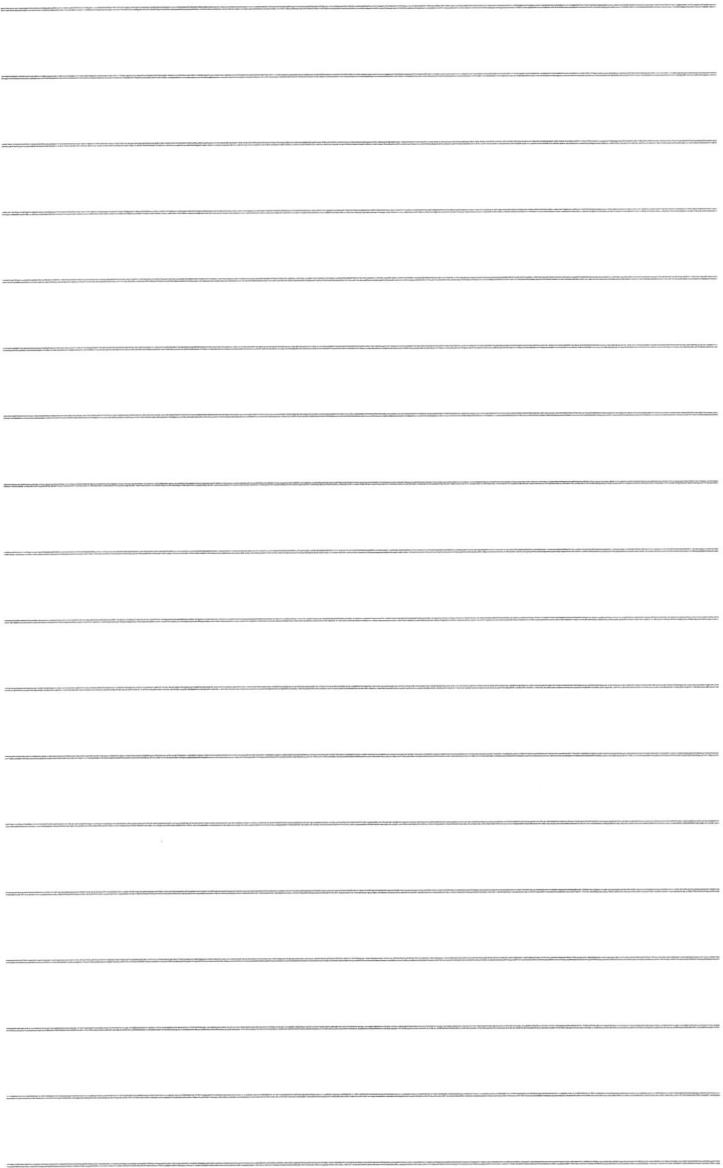

ACKNOWLEDGEMENTS

Huge thank you to my amazing Editor, Jordan Merritt, who took the time to comb through my book and keep it real with me about what needed to change/ what was amazing! I truly appreciate your time and diligence and for just truly being an amazing friend and editor!

Thank you to my contributors who opened up and told their stories about their struggles and successes of transitioning from college to adulthood. You all truly hold a special place in my heart and I am so thankful for your willingness to voluntarily let everyone into your experiences!

Thank you to Mercy B. Carruthers for originally planting the seed in me to write a book and tell my story. (Instagram: Mercybcarruthers).

Thank you to Dr. Fred Jones for leading a powerful class and emphasizing the need to Write my Worth!